Vicky the Vet

Felicity Brooks

Illustrated by Jo Litchfield

Designed by Nickey Butler

Veterinary Consultant:
Julie Saxton MA. VetMB. CertSAC. MRCVS

Veterinary Clinic

This is the clinic where Vicky the Vet works. Her job is to treat sick and injured animals. It's a sunny morning and some pets are arriving with their owners.

Today Vicky is working with Asha, the nurse and Sally, the receptionist.

Vicky

Asha

Sally

2

They take a quick look at the appointments book.
"Looks like a busy day," laughs Sally.

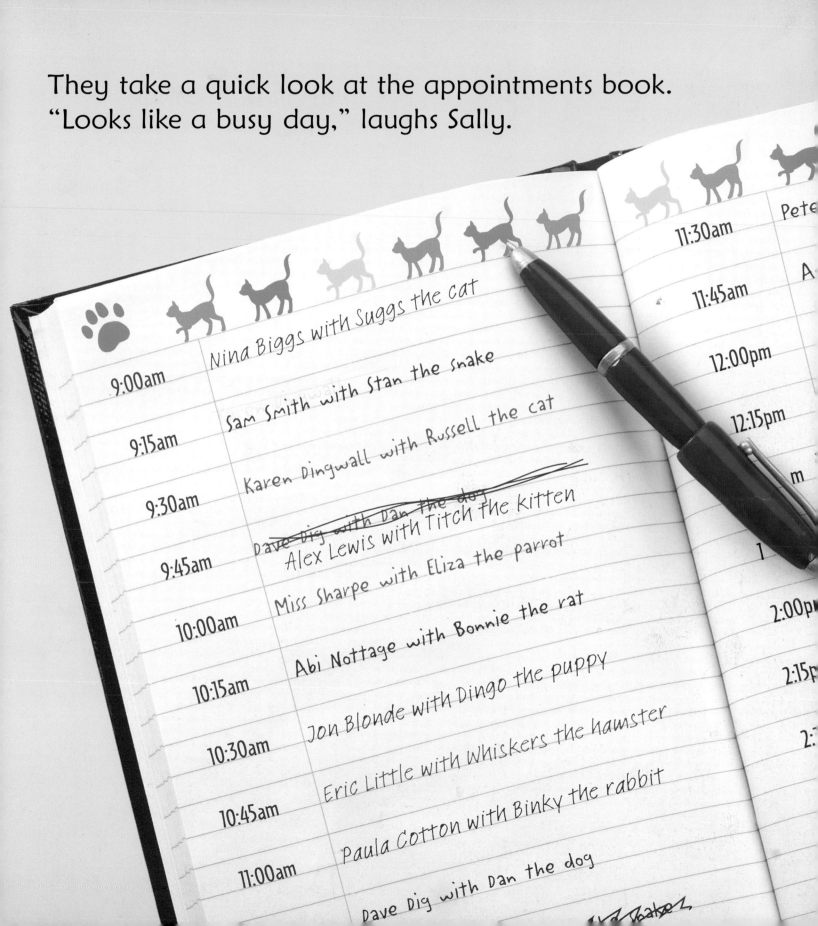

9:00am — Nina Biggs with Suggs the cat

9:15am — Sam Smith with Stan the snake

9:30am — Karen Dingwall with Russell the cat

9:45am — ~~Dave Dig with Dan the dog~~ Alex Lewis with Titch the kitten

10:00am — Miss Sharpe with Eliza the parrot

10:15am — Abi Nottage with Bonnie the rat

10:30am — Jon Blonde with Dingo the puppy

10:45am — Eric Little with Whiskers the hamster

11:00am — Paula Cotton with Binky the rabbit

Dave Dig with Dan the dog

11:30am — Pete
11:45am — A
12:00pm
12:15pm — m
2:00p
2:15p
2:

Vicky and Asha get ready for their first patient.

At nine on the dot Nina Biggs comes in. She looks worried.

"This is Suggs," she says. "He's got a bad paw and he's been yowling and howling all night."

Vicky asks Nina to put Suggs on the table. She strokes him gently and talks to him quietly. Asha holds up the bad paw for Vicky to examine.

"I think he's been bitten," Vicky explains, "and the wound's infected. You'll need to clean it like this every day."

"And give him one antibiotic tablet twice a day. He should start to feel better soon."

Outside, the waiting
room is packed.

Suddenly the front door swings open and in charges a man carrying a big dog. "My dog's been hit by... by... by a car," he pants. "Please help her!"

They rush the dog into the vet's room and Vicky uses her stethoscope to listen to its heart. The dog is shivering and cannot stand up.

"What's her name?" Vicky asks.
"Fudge," says the man anxiously.
"She will be all right, won't she?"

Vicky checks Fudge's breathing with her stethoscope.

She looks in her mouth and takes her pulse.

She checks her body all over for wounds and broken bones.

"Well," says Vicky at last, "I can't say just yet. She's very bruised and shocked, so we'll have to keep her here for treatment. She'll need a drip, some painkillers and other medicines."

"And then she'll have to have an X-ray," Vicky adds. "I'll call you later to let you know how she's doing."

"Poor dog," says Asha
as she helps carry
Fudge to the kennels.

Vicky's next patient is a little more unusual. It's a snake named Stan.

"I'm really worried," says Sam, the snake's owner. "His skin's all dry and his eyes look weird."

11

Vicky examines Stan and asks Sam questions.
"How long have you had him?"
"Just a couple of months," says Sam.

"He looks fine," says Vicky.
"He's just getting ready to shed his skin."

Because Stan is about to shed his skin, it looks very dull and his eyes are cloudy.

Soon Stan will wiggle out of his old skin. It will fold back and inside out.

12

The skin he leaves behind will look like a papery tube.

Stan will have shiny new skin.

"Now that he's grown up, he'll shed his skin like a sock every few months," Vicky explains.

"Make sure he's warm and has a big bowl of water in his tank. Soon he'll have nice new skin."
"Thanks," says Sam. "I will."

Just then there's a yell
from the waiting room.

"Rat on the loose!"
shouts Sally.

A girl is crawling around trying to catch her pet rat.

"He gnawed through the box," she wails as she tries to grab the rat.

They all try to catch the rat,

but he scurries through
a puppy's legs...

...and scuttles
around a cat
carrier...

...and scampers over a woman's feet...

...and scrambles
into her bag.

"Got him!" says Asha, throwing a towel over the bag.

She puts the rat in another box and hands him back to his owner. "What a morning," laughs Vicky.

Vicky sees lots more patients that day:

Dan the dog has fleas.

Binky the rabbit has a problem with her teeth.

Dingo the puppy needs a vaccination.

Whiskers the hamster has an eye infection.

Bonnie the rat has a lump on her cheek.

Eliza the parrot has hurt her wing.

Three tortoises named Bernie, Barry and Bob all have worms.

Russell the cat keeps scratching his ears.

Snowy the cat's teeth need cleaning.

Titch the kitten keeps sneezing.

Later, Vicky goes to check Fudge's X-ray.
Luckily there's nothing broken.

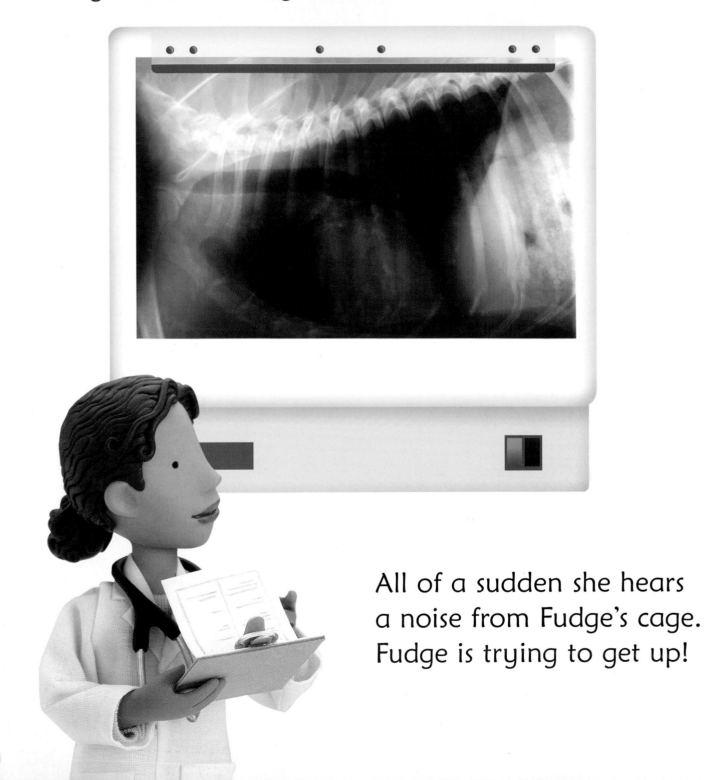

All of a sudden she hears
a noise from Fudge's cage.
Fudge is trying to get up!

"Hello girl," says Vicky. "We were all so worried about you." Fudge thumps her tail on her bed.

After she's checked Fudge again, Vicky calls her owner.

"Fudge is OK," she says, "but we'll need to keep an eye on her tonight."

"Thanks so much," says the owner. "We'll come and see her tomorrow."

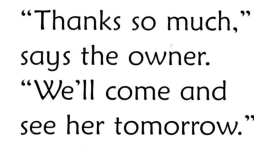

At last it's time for Vicky to go home.
"See you in the morning," she calls.

"For another busy day," laughs Sally.
"Bye bye!"

Vet words

Antibiotic – a type of medicine that kills tiny germs called bacteria.

Appointment – If you make an appointment, you arrange to see someone or be somewhere at a certain time.

Clinic – a place where doctors or vets see their patients.

Drip – a bag containing liquid that goes into the blood of a sick person or animal.

Fleas – tiny jumping insects that can live on animals and bite them.

Infected – If a wound is infected, it has lots of tiny germs called bacteria in it.

Infection – when lots of tiny germs called bacteria get into a part of an animal's or person's body.

Kennels – a place with lots of cages for animals to stay in.

Painkiller – a type of medicine that stops things from hurting.

Patient – an animal or person who goes to a vet or doctor for treatment.

Pulse – the throbbing you can feel in a vein as blood is pumped around a person's or animal's body.

Receptionist – the person at a doctor's or vet's clinic who makes the appointments.

Stethoscope – an instrument for listening to an animal's or person's breathing or heartbeat.

Treatment – all the things a vet or doctor does to help a sick animal or person get better.

Vaccination – using a needle to put medicine into an animal's or person's blood to stop them from catching a disease.

Worms – small animals that can live inside another animal and can make it ill.

X-ray – a picture of the inside of a person's or animal's body.

Photography: MMStudios

With thanks to Staedtler UK for providing the
Fimo® material for models,
and to Beaumont Veterinary Hospital, Oxford, UK

www.usborne.com
First published in 2004 by Usborne Publishing Ltd.,
Usborne House, 83-85 Saffron Hill, London EC1N 8RT, England. Copyright © 2004 Usborne Publishing Ltd.